The Hill
&
Other
Musings

Bill Erickson

The Hill
&
Other
Musings

Bill Erickson

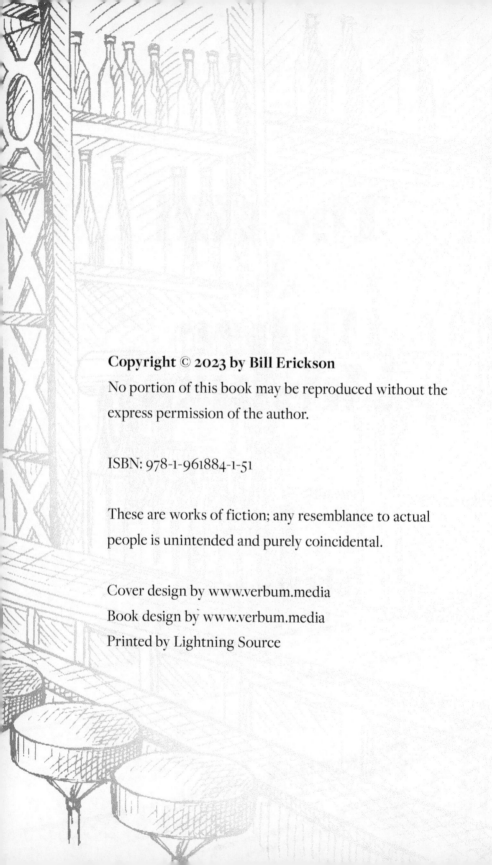

ISBN: 978-1-961884-1-51

These are works of fiction; any resemblance to actual people is unintended and purely coincidental.

Cover design by www.verbum.media
Book design by www.verbum.media
Printed by Lightning Source

Table of Contents

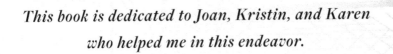

This book is dedicated to Joan, Kristin, and Karen
who helped me in this endeavor.

I am grateful to friend Sarah Maney
for her description of her poetry as "musings."
She taught me what I was doing
with these pages.

The Hill

*Snapshots from a sports bar
in the midcentury Midwest*

The Hill

A joint's a joint, say many who tip a beer.
Anybody who has been to the Hill knows better.
Lefty named the place the Hill very simply
because he pitched for the Elks from a hill
instead of a mound. That was his place of work.
When he retired from baseball, a monied friend
financed this special place of work for Lefty
which he quickly established into Bailey's Hill.
Sport celebrities and their followers were
the first to join Lefty as customers.
It didn't take long for a combination
of good story and drink to bring a throng.
For the first ten years, Lefty's generosity
impeded economic prosperity for the business.
It was a fun place and nearly always full,
but drinks on the house didn't fill the register.
Then Elly found the place!

Elmira "Elly" Bailey

Elly has owned the Hill for ten years.
She inherited it from "Lefty" Sam Bailey.
That's the short of it, but not the story.
In 1948 Elly Schmidt was the star
waitress at the Hill attracting customers
and capturing the heart of old Lefty.
They had married in 1950, when he
was 50, and they had run the Hill
in fun and frolic until he died in August, 1978.
Elly was proud that her husband had been
the all-time winningest lefthander
for the Elks over a career of 15 seasons.
He had set up the Hill the year he retired.
No one knew that the bar never made
money until the place found Elly.
She made all the difference, and her life
changed with Lefty's passing, but the
prosperity at the Hill never missed a beat.
Elly Bailey is a working tavern keeper
who believes in first count and last count.
She knows her patrons are the real owners,
and treats them like royalty and her staff
as associates in joint enterprise.
Lefty started and named the place.

He and Elly built the joint in their image.

Now Elly runs the place in the same

youthful exuberance she brought to it in '48.

Harold "Pop" Stein

Harold had been a bartender for Lefty

before Elly joined the staff at the Hill.

Somewhere along the way he became Pop.

His always thinning, greying hair and

old folks' mannerisms fit the name.

He always played big brother to other employees.

Off duty, Pop drank too much, but he bothered no one, so

it didn't interfere at work.

He kept his drinking on the right side of the bar.

Pop has been a loner but never lonely.

The Hill and staff have been home and family.

Stan Wolinski

A handsome man from the Polish northside
who had earned the nickname "Stud" through
his experience and reputation with the "ladies."
Stan is a bartender's specimen at an age, 27,
when most have not combined gifts of gab and dexterity.
When working, he is the centerpiece at the Hill,
a major sports bar hang-out for all the movers.
It seems he's behind the bar most of the time
except when the Hill's amateur softball team plays,
then he pitches and bats clean-up as a champion.
Stan can talk sports with customers in all seasons,
but he is also knowledgeable with public events.
He is clever-funny without being obscene or bitter,
and has a poetic way with words that pleases women.
He is respected highly by his boss for his honesty
        and ability,
and by the waitresses for his helpful protective cover.
Stan is so good that he figures that his tip pot
will be big enough within three years to finance
"Stan's Place," the watering hole of his dream.
Mr. Pretty Pole, how do you fit?

Candace Sims

Except for Elly herself, Candy is the
only lady to serve behind the bar at the Hill.
She started five years ago as a waitress,
and went to bar tending school to qualify.
Pop Stein really taught her the important things
that made her the outstanding bar keep she is.
Candy has made a practice to never date
any of the guys who are Hill regulars.
This has been troublesome, because she is a
pretty gal and very attractive to men.
She has always managed an active social life
in spite of the fact that she keeps it away from her job.

Shelly Mink

Shelly has been at the Hill a couple years,
and her waitress station is always the most fun.
She is always surprised, when she is often asked,
"What are you doing in a job like this?"
She liked the Hill, the folks who worked there,
most of the people she served, and, significantly,
she made more money than the askers could guess.
After two years at college, and two more in an
office, she had found her work-home at the Hill.

Pete Petsch

Pete started working at the Hill a year ago part-time,

while taking a full-time schedule of classes at the U.

Now he is only part-time student and will be full-time

at the Hill as soon as he is hired as bar tender.

Nothing about school interests him as much as working

behind the bar for the patrons who come to the Hill.

He knows he has much to learn and he is willing.

Henry Prairie

Henry is quite a dapper old fellow

who appears late afternoon once or twice a week.

He usually wears a casual sweater

with slacks and has a brandy or two, leisurely.

Frenchy doesn't talk much, but when

he does, the accent shows the reason for his nickname.

Most of the folks don't realize that

Henry is the swamper for the Hill, and has been for years.

He was a bar tender for Lefty, but

used too much of the sauce himself, on the job.

Lefty never could fire "friends" so

he made French the janitor twenty years ago.

Elly has kept him on for Lefty, and,

incidentally, because he keeps the place like his own.

Robert J. Brown

Today Robert is an outstanding insurance marketer
who does much of his business at the Hill.
He is one of the top producers for his company,
and high in leadership in our city's Black community.
In the late 30's he was a bar boy for Lefty
while he worked his way through the University.
"Shine" he answered to at the Hill until he returned
as a Captain in the Air Corps during World War II.
When he settled back home after his discharge,
it was Robert, or Mr. Brown, and Bob only from
close friends.
This identity was established while still keeping close
friendship with Elly and Lefty, until Lefty died.
He credited them as sponsors of his education,
and is comfortable as a regular Hill patron.
His clientele is multiracial, so he has had a big part
in making and keeping the Hill truly integrated.
Elly credits Bob with teaching her staff the
right way to deal with all people, and, thereby,
making the Hill a comfortable place for all patrons.

Horace P. Sampson

Horace made his money in the trucking business,

and he has owned the Cats, our NBA franchise, for

thirty years.

As a friend, he financed Lefty into the Hill at the start.

He regularly came in the Hill for years, but now

not so often, because his ball players frequent the place.

Lefty liked and respected Horace, but Elly thought

Evelyn Sampson a snob, so the couples were not friendly.

Still every ten years or so, when the Cats would win the

division, the celebration was always at the Hill.

Evelyn Sampson

Mrs. Sampson never liked Lefty, even before the Hill.

She could not understand why her husband had

any connection.

Whenever Horace wanted her with him there,

she resisted.

Most of all, she couldn't stand Elly, but of course being

the lady she is, she never showed her feelings, she thought.

Evelyn had borne six young Sampsons and been married

to Horace for forty-five years. That was enough!

Horace P. (Paul) Sampson, Jr.

The first born – and a son at that.

Paul was and is all you can ask, as parents.

Proper and diligent at school, dutiful at home.

Now at forty-three, his BA and MBA

place him at his father's right hand in all affairs.

As a boy he knew the Hill when Horace visited

Lefty on Saturday afternoons. It was fun.

As a young man he enjoyed the special

uncle-nephew relationship with Lefty.

It was a special place to relax and unwind –

until his brother Roger came of age.

Roger Sampson

Roger is the spoiled youngest of three boys.

At thirty, he has one younger and two older sisters.

He took six years to almost get through the U.

His dad has been "bringing him into the trucking,"

but it has not much interrupted his play.

Roger enjoys the Hill very much, except

the rare occasions his father is around.

He makes a bit of a fool of himself with the

ladies, but he is quiet, respectful and tips well.

Caran Sampson

Caran is the youngest of Horace and Evelyn's brood.
She has been just as spoiled as Roger, and three
years younger.
The result is very different, however. She is a dear.
School was finished on schedule with excellent grades.
Her degree in Humanities at the U. came with honors.
Her time at the Hill is fun, but its purpose is to
try to influence Roger, and that is where she finds him.

Jill Butts

Jill was a classmate and sorority sister of Caran Sampson
at the U. She didn't know the Sampson family at all
until she moved to the city a little less than a year ago.
Six months ago, she was at the Hill with Caran when her
life's purpose changed as she was introduced to
brother Roger.

He was for her, in her mind, and she began her attack.

Tony Andreo

Tony is the Bud distributor to the Hill.

His dad, Tony, also set Lefty up at the start.

Tony, Sr., taught Lefty about the bar business.

Because of that, Budweiser products have

always been featured at the Hill Bar.

Tony can remember coming into the place

as a teenager, making deliveries for his dad.

It was a favorite spot before his dad died,

twelve years ago, and it remains his best customer.

Elly still is more like family than customer.

Lois Willow

Twenty-seven years ago, she was born Wilofski.
She is still a proud Pole, but changed her name.
Lois is a reporter for the local CBS outlet,
and Willow fits better for an aspiring anchor.
She became acquainted with the Hill because
her court house beat often took her there.
There is no better talent with energy in town.
She works at her networking and seems to
have a sixth sense for sources on a scoop.
But presentation on the air is her real forte.
She is just a short step from her anchor goal.

Zia Johnson

This lady is something other than ordinary.
A lovely thirty-year-old woman who works
with Lois Willow at WNCP as a reporter.
Zia was a brilliant kid from South Carolina
who found herself at Wellesley on Merit Scholarship.
After finishing college with distinction, she
worked as a reporter for Newsweek before coming
to our county five years ago for life in TV.
Lois brought her to the Hill when she first arrived.
Now she comes around quite often, evenings,
with a number of friends, mixed in age, sex, and race,
but interestingly, never includes Lois Willow.
Miss Johnson expects the next anchor spot herself.

Linden Rutherford

Lin came to the practice of law seven years ago.
That was the same time he began playing at the Hill.
Between practice and play, he has had no time
for marriage.
He is a good young lawyer with Swift and Vanevery.
His future specialty he intends to be representation
of professional athletes, and proudly joins Brad Pell
on Lois Willow's network of sources for news tips.
Linden is certain that his interest in that reporter
can be developed into a serious relationship.

Bradley Pell

Poor greying, balding, fattening Bradley –
He is Clerk of District Court by reason of skill.
Brad was reporter for the senior judge when the
former Clerk died, so Brad got the appointment.
He sees a lot of Lois Willow in her networking.
His hopes for more than her business are groundless.
After forty-one years a bachelor, he expects no more.

Mildred Bumsey

Assistant City Clerk is a big job in our town.

Millie is the first female to ever hold the position.

She started in the Clerk's office twenty years ago.

It was her first job out of high school and

she has held the city's top non-political spot two years.

Mildred is good in the office, but one of the guys away.

She has always joined the group on the fifteenth and

month's end with new paychecks for a visit to the Hill.

Dancy Burns

Twenty years ago, his peak was number three ranked
welter weight.
He fought some of the best, but never for
the championship.
His father was his manager, so unlike most
        former fighters,
he has some money, and his brain and body still function.
Dancy probably makes as much money these days on
TV commercials as he did in the ring at his best.
Every week he comes in the Hill with people from
boxing, folks he works with, or cronies from high school.
Dancy Burns is one of the nice things about the Hill.

Mike Carlo

Mike comes into the Hill a couple of times a day
when Lydall Shoe Store is open across the way.
He fits ladies' feet with charm and style
that keeps him leading salesman at Lydall.
He has a beer for a morning or afternoon lift,
and a bump, with his beer, at the end of the shift.
Regular he is, but never for long.
His New Jersey accent is very strong,
and he is proud of his Italian heritage.
No one belittles him about his parentage.

Harold Van Boyle

Some people are funny and some are comedians.

Harold Van Boyle is a laughing riot when he visits the Hill.

He must weigh three hundred pounds on his 5'10" frame,

and he looks like a big round butter ball.

Somewhere along the way, Harold learned to live

with himself by learning to laugh at himself.

When he comes in with his bunch from City Hall,

Hal not only entertains them but turns most

heads around.

Hi Dickman

Hi writes a sports column for the Telegraph.
He is knowledgeable about athletics in all respects,
as anyone should being around for thirty years.
He often claims that his custom and interviews
of sport celebrities was the making of the Hill.
Old regulars know better. He didn't even come
in town until long after Elly graced the place.
Hi is important to the business, because
he is well known and friendly to the house.
His word has been accepted many times to
settle sports arguments otherwise disruptive.

Cynthia Anderson

Cindy has always liked jocks.
People at the Hill aren't bothered
because she isn't a professional.
When she started coming in the place
six years ago, she was an attractive kid.
Now, she is a jaded groupie of twenty-four
who attracts none of the new guys anymore.
She has no friends who come in with her.
It seems she knows just when
athletes are going to be present.
She is around the Hill no other time.
So far as anyone knows, no guy
living in town has ever left with her.
She likes guys from visiting teams.

Mike Ryan

Handsome, quick, and always "cock of the walk."
Mike was a good high school athlete, who at
35, still carries himself and looks like one.
He left his small town after high school and
was further educated in the school of hard knocks,
via door-to-door selling books, all over the country;
vacuum cleaner sales, when he married 14
years ago, so that he could stay in our city;
real estate sales for the last ten years, which
contributed to his divorce three years ago.
He always led in sales and made money easily,
and provided well, beyond court orders, for his three
boys, who live with their remarried mother.
As a non-church-going Catholic, Mike lives
comfortably with all persons in the community.
He considers himself a first-class real estate
professional, ready for "big time" development, and
those who know him best are ready to back him.

Paul "Hunk" Tobler

Paul is and always has been a hunk.
He played ten years in the NFL,
the last seven with our Bison.
Hunk was an All-American defensive end
at Alabama, and played tackle as a pro.
When he retired in 1985, he entered the
real estate business with Mike Ryan.
They had met at the Hill ten years ago.
At six foot six and two hundred and eighty pounds,
this agent makes quite an impression.
His southern speech and charm backed by a
well-educated intelligence and good work ethic
guarantee success under Mike's tutelage.
Hunk is a rare one – his brain in the market
is worth as much as his brawn was on the field.

Hope Sewell

There are people who look much the same all the time.
Some others appear not the same on any two occasions.
Hope Sewell is one of the latter. Some days she appears
at the Hill as a strikingly beautiful young lady, and
the next as a not very pretty, tough broad off the street.
The change is so dramatic that she regularly is not
recognized by people who see her often but don't
know her.

Hope has been coming to the Hill for about three years,
since she started working for Mike Ryan in real estate.
That association has been rewarding for both of them.
She is happier and making more money than she did
as a school teacher before joining Mike's operation.
But, her one failed marriage has not dimmed her
romantic interest, and for three years it aimed at Mike.

Allen Sundt

The place kicker for the bison lived in the city.

He was a quiet man, who liked the last bar stool;

just as he regularly sat at the end of the Bison bench.

He visited the Hill often, in and out of football season.

Sometimes he came with a lady (different ones),

but most of the time he as alone, even when

some of his team mates were in the bar.

Kickers are a little strange, everyone thought, so

most of the time he was left by himself.

Rich Simpson

A slick fielding, long ball hitting first baseman
was what the Elks called up from triple A, May, 1982.
Edward Richard (Rich) Simpson has owned Elk's first
base ever since, batting over 290 and winning two
gold gloves.
Rich is a celebrity-regular at the Hill, and is often
joined in frolic there by his wife Lynn and friends.
He learned baseball in the fast high school and legion
leagues of Fresno, California, and college at Stanford.
At Stanford he was All-American on the diamond, and
was graduated, unathlete-wise, in four years.
With the Elks, he is a team leader, on and off field.
For our community, Rich and Lynn are good citizens.
The powers on the club expect him to play for some
time more, but Rich is already looking for life
after baseball.

Lynn Simpson

Lynn was born a Torgerson in Little Chicago, Minn.,

and was a reporter for KDRD-TV for two years

before she met and married her husband in 1985.

She continues her career, but her husband

and prospective family are her personal aspirations.

To her, Rich is a good man and good husband,

who temporarily plays first base for a living.

They live in a glare, but she, too, looks forward,

with calmness to married life after baseball.

"Ace" Rank

Ace has been a regular at the Hill
for longer than anyone knows.
He is familiar with most of the people
who come there, but no one knows him,
his real first name, or what he does.
Ace is a good listener, pays his bar bill
and is a generous tipper, so he is always
welcome with everyone in the place.
He has been seen, at one time or other,
by other regulars, with all the other folks
that make up the custom of the house.
he looks to be in his well-kept late 50's,
always nicely dressed, and is around
so much, everyone knows he has money.
If he has a wife, no one has seen her.
If he has a family, no one has heard about them.
The liberals around the place believe he is also,
and the conservatives know he is one of them.
Ace is like non-glare glass on a picture,
supporting to the scene but unobtrusive.

Brunhilde Benson

She was a cute kid, pretty teenager, and
now, at forty, is a striking blond who does up well.
Brunhilde is a big woman, in stature, talent,
will, energy and especially in relationship.
She is neither lady nor tart but plays both easily.
Her intelligence has been well educated through public
schools, the University of Minnesota, and an
18-year experience with advertising and media.
B.B. has had considerable commercial success,
which has kept her single and near the top financially.
She has bruised through the years tasting of
things and people but has not taken time to
know any of them – things or people.
Can love and happiness come to this dynamo
with an unlikely college major of history?

Louis P. O'Neil

Lou O'Neil is not your typical recovering hard drinker.
Matter of fact, he is not typical in any way.
He doesn't drink anymore, and hasn't for his last
eight years, because the doctor who did his heart surgery
told him he would die if he didn't stop. He did --
cold turkey.
Doesn't sound like much, but Lou was a magic drinker.
He just got funnier and wiser the more he drank,
and he always drank a lot. He loved the smell, the
taste, the crowd, and no one recalls one scene
of drunkenness.
Lou was and is one of our most successful trial lawyers.
He is magic in court rooms for many of the same
reasons he is famous at the Hill, charm and grace,
but mostly because he is so good with juries.
Lou still frequents the Hill, probably as much as ever,
because he still likes the smell and the crowd.
He simply doesn't drink because he knows he'd die.
Most of the people who come in the Hill don't
even realize that he isn't drinking booze.
This carefully dressed man, in his early sixties,
always has a drink in his hand, near the center
of whatever action there is at the Hill, when he is there.
Lou tells how he even found and won his wife

of thirty years, at the Hill during his "salad years."
Sally still comes in with him, at least once a well.
He sings the songs in his glorious Irish tenor,
tells stories with the best, and waits for the day he is
told he is going to die, so he can drink again.

Sally Johnson O'Neil

It was almost thirty years ago Sally Johnson
first came into the Hill with friends from the U.
That first time she saw Lou O'Neil carrying on,
and, on the spot, she knew she had to have him.
It was a piece of cake the way the pretty little
farm girl swept the barrister off his feet in no time.
The twelve years difference in age has tantalized.
Sally has loved him dearly, borne their four children,
Mary, now 28, named for his mother; Richard, twenty-six;
Ted, almost 25, and their youngest, Roger, twenty.
Sally fell in love with a singing poet in a bar.
Every year she has grown to love him more.

Dee Dee Sims

She was born in 1948, the year Bebe Shopp was
Miss America.
Her mother thought Dee Dee looked and sounded better.
Dee Dee wasn't slowed by her name in the least.
She was the youngest person ever named head nurse
at our General Hospital and she earns it every day.
The Hill has been the gathering spot at least once a week
since Dee Dee was a student there twenty years ago.
Before she was legal, she joined the General gang,
and has been coming regularly ever since then.

Howard Dumpas

Howard was the youngest boy in the state

to win the Boy Scout badge of the Eagle.

He was, and still is an Eagle Scout in all respects.

As coach of the Hill softball team, he is able,

so his being good is suffered in silence.

You would think he coached grammar school

instead of young men playing for a tavern.

But, year after year, he enlists and manages

a team that wins games and plays as champions.

For twenty-five years the Hill has been sponsor.

Professionally, Howard is a geologist who

has worked for the state supervising mining.

Eddie Dumpas

Eighteen years ago, when he was eight, his dad started
bringing him to the games he coached for the Hill.
For the last nine years he has caught for the club.
Eddie did not win Eagle, or even Life for that matter.
He finished high school at Central, in a fashion,
but he was a student like his mom, not his dad.
Howard is proud of him, because he works hard as a
roofer and is steady in support of his wife and family.
Eddie is proud to play for his dad for the Hill.
Father and son contribute greatly to the softball wins.

Harry Mankiewitz

Harry is the Hill's resident bookie.
All the regulars know that. Some bet with him.
He has been coming to the Hill for over
twenty years, long before Lefty passed away.
Lefty and Elly have had an absolute against
prostitutes and bookies in their place.
But Harry Mankiewitz is smooth and slick.
He had been a regular for several years before
it was commonly known what he did,
and he never did anything at the Hill.
By that time, he was a good friend to Lefty,
Elly, and most of the regulars in the place.
Tell Lefty, before he died, or Elly, now,
that Harry is taking bets. "Nonsense" either
would have responded, and gone about business.

Dale Hyslop

A couple of times a month Dale runs

friendly 5K and 10K races where he finds them.

He promises to run the Boston Marathon one day.

He races wearing a T-shirt printed Flying Bachelor.

Dale is a practicing C.P.A., with a big 8 firm.

Every day, after work, regardless of weather, he runs

a couple of miles over down town streets to the Hill

where he stops for a beer before walking home to shower.

Needless to say, over the five years of this pattern

he has become a celebrity at the Hill.

Some of the regulars follow him to his races.

Some of the ladies even follow him to other places.

Judy Shea

Judy works for the telephone company, customer service.
At least a couple of times a week she and her friends
go across the street to the Hill after they leave work.
That silly runner fellow, Dale Hyslop, has made
their visits more interesting than might have been so.
At first Judy was intrigued by the fellow's practice.
Then she was interested in his personality.
She believes she has piqued his interest as well.
She and her friend, Brenda Starz, have been
going to some of Dale's races for the last year.
Dale usually sits with them when he is at
the Hill, and meets them after his races for a beer.
The problem is that Judy is afraid that Brenda
has the same interest in following Dale, as she does.

Darling Don

Don Woody, born Donald Wodiehowski,

is pro wrestling's pretty boy, Darling Don.

He is a contender for the local circuit's championship.

Don has been wrestling professionally for four years,

and has been a feature at the Hill for longer than that.

Actually, he grew up on the North Side

two houses from his cousin, Stan Wolinski.

Stan's mom and his are sisters, and Stan has

always been an influence, and not always good.

Stan did enlist him as catcher and clean up

hitter for the Hill softball team before he was a star.

You can understand, when Don is catching,

opposing teams are not inclined to brawl.

Sue Woody

Sue met Don Wodiehowski at North High when
he was a junior and she was a sophomore.
They were a steady pair through high school
and Don's first two years at the University.
Sue took a one-year business school course,
and then went to work for her dad, Stu Maki.
She took over the office for Stu's station
Whirlwind Gasoline and Convenience Company.
Don and Sue could afford to marry before his
junior year at the U., and also work for Stu.
The diminutive Sue, all five-foot one-inch,
one hundred pounds rules her wrestler carefully.
You can imagine his two hundred sixty on a
six-foot three-inch frame walking with her.
They are quite a pair at the Hill.

Debra Maki

Deb is Sue Woody's older sister by two years.
After her teaching degree, she returned to North High
to teach social studies to the tenth graders there.
In the Maki family, Sue got the looks and Deb
got the brains, and both were jealous of the other.
Deb enjoyed her students and teaching, but felt
that there was more to life than her pupils.
She much enjoyed the camaraderie of the Hill
when she could join her sister and Don there.
She kept hoping that one of those big friends of
Don's would take an interest in Sue's brainy sister.

Deidre

She always saw things differently.

Her hearing was excellent also.

She heard things others didn't hear.

Color and sound mixed in her head.

Imagination is a blessing to an artist,

but Deidre was just a secretary.

They said she had bats in her belfry.

Robert H. Witt

Bob Witt is truly a local kid who made it.

He started playing trumpet at South High '62.

He honed his skill at the Cincinnati Conservatory,

playing in the Cincinnati and New York Orchestras.

He now is the principal trumpet for our Symphony.

Bob started coming to the Hill when he returned

to town in 1976 because of sport celebrities.

Through his interest in participatory athletics

he has been used often as a side attraction

at most of the stadiums and arenas in town.

He plays the meanest Mozart concerto but

also makes the trumpet sing for the commoners, too.

Bob and his wife, Hildy, class up the Hill.

Hildema Witt

Hildy joined Bob at the Cincinnati Conservatory
where she was studying piano in his class.
She still plays for her own enjoyment, gives
lessons for about ten hours a week for pin money,
and sometimes, in fun, pounds on the Hill piano.
Her one child, Robert, Jr., is a non-musician,
senior in accounting at the University.
Hildy loves her husband and shares in many
of his interests including, of course, his music.
His interests in athletics she couldn't appreciate
until she also fell in love with the Hill folks.

Hope Sargeant

Whatever happens to those former cheer leaders?
Hope was with the Bison dance line twenty years ago.
She started coming to the Hill back then and since.
When she danced and cheered the Bison, her name
was Jackson and she has had two other name changes.
Each of her three husbands has been known at the Hill,
and, interestingly enough, to each other, as well.
Hope remains a sophisticated marvel of our time.
She has no children, not worked since college,
continues to look strikingly gorgeous on her Hill visits
and keeps on friendly basis with each of her three
husbands, before, during and after each marriage.

Allen Anderson

In the Upper Midwest everyone knows an
Allen Anderson.
As a matter of fact, it's a common name all over.
This Allen Anderson is a representative for Rogers & Co.,
one of the liquor distributors supplying booze to the Hill.
Allen tries usually to make a last call of the day at the Hill.
He likes to have a drink or two before heading to
his home.
This pattern was set during his first year at Rogers
in 1963.
He's a good rep for his company and he likes the business.
Al doesn't think it matters that Eloise Anderson was
born Rogers.
That is not the view of most of the folks who know Allen.
The Hill patrons know him as a supplier who sets up
for the bar when he comes in a couple of times a month.

Eloise Anderson

Eloise loves her husband of twenty-six years,
and is very proud of their five children.
Her dad had made a pile in the liquor trade.
Eloise only has one sibling, a brother, Roger,
who is five years younger than her and her Allen.
It has ceased to bother Eloise, that her brother,
and not her husband, now manages Rogers & Company.
Her Allen is satisfied being a rep for the company.
Compensation had been more than adequate
and ultimately half the wealth will be hers also.
Her only real pain is the once every month
or so that she must rescue Allen from the Hill.
She believes that it must be a very bad place
because Allen has never strayed anywhere else.

Allen R. Anderson, Jr. (Buck)

Buck has always appreciated his nickname
because he has never liked to be called Junior.
He likes being named after his dad because they're close.
His father has always had lots of time for and with him.
As the oldest of five and only Son, it seemed natural.
They hunted, went to ballgames, visited places,
and did many things few of his friends' fathers shared.
His dad had taught him much, but he especially
respected what his attitude was about use of alcohol.
Allen, Sr. always talked with him about drinking,
but he never drove after more than two drinks.
At twenty-one, Buck had learned how to enjoy the
use of booze without losing sight of potential abuse.
Buck understood and appreciated why his dad
would call for a ride from the Hill, and he
never could understand his mother's attitude.

Judge Jessica Hanson

Jessica started in the County Attorney's office
when she finished college in the spring of '52.
She worked as a secretary while going to law
school nights for the necessary four years.
When she was sworn in to practice, it was
a simple switch for her to become prosecutor.
Twenty years ago, she was the first lady
appointed to the Bench in our community.
Judge Jess is a hard worker, a good judge.
She started coming to the Hill with the crowd.
She still comes, once in a while, as one of the guys.

Thomas H. Tudley

T.T. or Teets is what he's called at the Hill,
and everywhere else for that matter since childhood.
He's a wonder to the Hill and the whole city.
T.T. went to high school in Asparagus, Wisconsin
with Burt Ramseth, one of our multi-millionaires.
He went to our university with him and has been
with him ever since as the highest paid gopher in town.
Mr. Tudley has an office in Ramseth's headquarters
in the Ramseth Tower, but most calls come to the Hill.
It seems he is around the Hill all the time
when he is not with Burt or on a mission for him.
He decorates the place, this handsome, greying, late
40's, trim fellow in his dark tailored outfits.

Steve Jordan

In high school Steve wrote sports for his school paper
and provided copy for his local weekly chronicle.
At St. Cloud State he wrote sports for four years.
For twenty years he has been on the baseball
beat for the Post after writing sports for the Air Force
Times for his two-year military hitch after college.
Steve is a fine writer and sports are his thing.
He is so narrow in his concentration that
he has lost two wives because of his dedication.
From spring training through the season, he
travels with the team, and lives with them at home.
His constant attention, on and off the field,
gains for Post readers an insight rare indeed.
Hill regulars see Steve more than any other writers,
but few know him. He keeps focused on ball players.

Richard C. Dunnell

Dick learned his reporting work habits from Steve Jordan.

When he finished the U. in journalism, he joined the Post.

He was assigned to sports and worked for his first

ten years very closely with Steve, even finding the Hill.

Two years ago, he was advanced to the City Desk.

This pleased him, since he wants to become an editor.

He doesn't miss his sports beat friends at all,

because he continues off-hour association at the Hill.

Mary Twining

As the only gal in the Post sports department
ten years ago, when she was hired, she covered all
girls' and women's sports, scholastic and college.
Now she is the senior of five female staffers.
Mary also does female sports for WCNP TV.
Steve Jordan and Dick Dunnell welcomed her
with a good bit of training after hours at the Hill.
Female athletics, at all levels, keeps increasing
in coverage in the media as competition grows.
Mary is pleased with the opportunity this provides,
and is very professionally taking advantage.

Father Pat Reardon

As a teenager, Pat Reardon was thought
to be a major league infield prospect.
The church won his attention, but baseball
has always been a consuming avocation.
For twenty-eight years a small committee
of his parishioners at St. Joseph's have given
him season tickets to the Elks games,
Father Pat visits the Hill in his Elks' ministry.

Mary Alice Reardon

Her uncle, Father Pat, taught her to love baseball,
and also introduced her to the fun of the Hill.
Mary's dad is Father Pat's younger brother and
her parents have always appreciated his care for Mary.
A young lady in the tow of a Catholic priest had
considerable advantages even if he is a different age.
Mary Alice learned much of life and baseball
that her plumber father and mother often knew not.

Edwin J. King

Hi, he is called. Short for His Highness
he acquired while in high school.
He is anything but regal, but his cab
is one of the busiest in the community.
Lefty used his cab for the last five years
of his life, whenever he went away from the Hill.
Hi made money with his cab. He carried
packages before it was the usual thing.
The highlight of his life was his friendship
with Lefty Bailey and Horace Sampson.

Hugh "Crusher" Gates

Any time Lefty and now Elly knew

a big bunch of outlanders would be at the Hill

after a game they would call Hugh Gates.

He had been the largest of the city's finest

for twenty years and a friend of Lefty's before.

At six foot six and two hundred-sixty pounds

he had little trouble maintaining order.

On the few occasions Hugh could not be

available his friend and fellow officer

Jim Lepcio would substitute for order.

Hugh had always spent as much time at

the Hill relaxing as he had maintaining peace.

James Lepcio "the Basher"

Jim was the second "man of peace" for the Hill.
Lefty had determined that strangers in his place
could be controlled by strict rules of conduct,
enforced at all times by his regular employees.
On the crowded times he wanted bouncers
to be so obvious that no one would fool with them.
He wanted them to look and dress as gentlemen,
but when called on as Basher or Crusher by
his associates, he wanted the point made.
Jim was slightly smaller than Hugh, but
obviously not a man to be taken lightly.
Like his fellow, he enjoyed the Hill off-duty, too.

Dr. Stuart W. Weingartner

His practice afforded time and money
to follow his interest in sport and athletics.
For twenty years he has regularly
attended games of football, basketball,
baseball, and hockey with his wife, Angela.
For the same period, they followed
the players in relaxation to the Hill.
A hero-worshiping professional man
and wife are interesting decorations.

Nancy Marsh

Here we have the proverbial big dumb blond.
This one, however, has gorgeous flaming red hair.
Really, she is quiet in a cultured way, even though
it seems her mouth is always slightly open,
and her eyes so wide they might be lost.
She need display no great intellect for her modeling.
Her physical beauty and structure qualify beyond.
The friends at the Hill worry constantly, because
she is the target of every guy that comes in the place.
There is no reason for concern, however.
She is as strong and discerning as she is beautiful.

Ira Johnson

Ira was a fine quarterback at the U. in the early '60s.
He was the first Black man to play that position in
the conference.
The Kings drafted him second in 1962 to play corner back,
and he was a fixture for eleven seasons on defense
for them.
As a player, Ira was always smart and dependable.
In school while other athletes were playing, he studied.
He learned about computers, and practiced while
playing football.
When he quit the Kings in 1973, he hit the road running.
He now has one of the largest software companies in
     the country,
specializing in product for churches and schools.
Ira is the All-American boy capping the dream.
At the Hill he shows a slightly different Ira Johnson.
He has a couple of beers with a party and lets his
hair down.
He laughs and scratches with the guys and puts on no airs.

Irene Drake

Irene is children's clothes buyer for Hannons.
There's usually a bunch from the store at the Hill
most every night after close, sometimes Irene.
She likes athletics. She played girls' basketball
in a small Iowa town twenty years ago.
The success that she has earned at her job
has not carried over to her private life – no guy.
Irene comes with the bunch and leaves with them.
Ellie Schmitt, a classmate from college, often
joins her group at the Hill, and is Irene's close friend.
Irene works hard with imagination and talent.
Other than that, she fills her life with her church,
work with the Republicans and trips to Iowa.

Elinor Schmitt

Elinor came to the city to go to law school.
She took a job as a legal secretary for money,
and started a four-year night law course.
She enjoyed her work in the law office.
Her law school didn't wear as well.
She got tired of the law all day and night,
and quit law school after a year and a half.
Elinor earns a good salary and, because she
performs so well, is paid a good bonus, too.
She enjoys going to the Hill with Irene
because Irene is attracted to men but
someone men don't find attractive.
Next to Irene, Elinor always looks good.
That's been true since college.
Ride a good horse 'til it drops.

Dan Swift

There aren't many left around anymore.

Dan was a young man when Lefty opened the door.

He's now one of the senior lawyers in the state,

but he still frequents the Hill at this late date.

The lawyers and judges that come to the Hill

very often are paid for on Dan Swift's bill.

William A. Vanevery

Bill or Van – he is called both –
was introduced to the Hill by Dan Swift.
Dan took him out for a beer after winning
a case where Van assisted at trial.
That was ten years ago, but Van still
practices law with the master and shares the Hill.
Unlike many of his trial lawyer friends, Van
is not a heavy drinker, but he enjoys comradery,
during and after the battle with his brethren.
For him the Hill is almost an extension office,
some of his best settlements have been made there.
He stops in three or four times a week, but
very often has a Coke, and never more than a beer.

Richard A. Turner

Dick was graduated from the U. Law School last June.

He joined Swift and Vanevery at the office and Hill.

He treats the Hill like a "club," and feels privileged

to be included with the lawyers joining Dan and Van.

He brings friends of his own to the Hill, only when

he is quite certain none of his firm will be there.

He has learned to emulate Van and not Dan

in the use of alcohol. He wants to be successful.

Dick was a good student and has been a quick learner.

If he has a weakness, it's his eye for the ladies.

Judge Jerome Winter

Before he was elevated to the bench
Jerry Winter was Dan Swift's partner.
The Honorable Judge Winter is still
Jerry around the bar at the Hill.
In his younger days, he was known
to have one too many on occasion.
The Judge is always very proper.

Amis "Preacher" Thomas

Amis got his nickname because of the way
he stands and poses over sacked quarterbacks.
Off the field, he is a well-spoken, gentle man.
In a Bison uniform he is among the sack leaders,
and he has played in the NFL only five years.
Amis makes his home here and enjoys his
leadership influence in our community.
Preacher and his wife, Roella, come to the Hill
only outside of football season, because
they feel they could influence young folks poorly.
The sterling graduate of Grambling fully
intends his impact on our city to be favorable.

Roella Thomas

Roella and Amis have been an "item"
since they were sophomores in college.
They were married the day of the draft,
when the Bison selected Amis number one.
Because of their special relationship, Amis'
move to the pros was smooth as silk.
Roella works full time, making life away
from the football fun and easy for her husband.
At the Hill she shows her lovely smiling face
always toward her husband and his friends.

Richard Kantorowicz

Dick is another of the Hill's "celeb" regulars.

His jobs include public address for the Elks,

a sports' beat for a radio station and MCing banquets.

He is a 55-year-old kid who wallows in sports.

His time at the Hill is spent with athletes

in spite of the fact, he uses no alcohol.

Dick is popular on the podium because he's trivia

smart and very quick with the humorous quip.

At the Hill, he can be found with a group talking

sports, at any time, but only if an athlete is present.

John Countryman

John played halfback for the U.
lots of years ago, 1958-1962.
He met Lefty when he started
coming into the Hill back then.
John never played professional football,
but he stayed in the game as an official.
He started officiating high school
games in all sports, and he was good.
It wasn't long before he was at the
college level and then the Big 10.
For the last ten years he has been
with the N.F.L., the last five years
as head man for one of its best crews.
John still comes into the Hill,
and is a popular figure at the bar.
His daytime job distributing beer
paid the bills for his family,
but he saw himself an NFL referee.

Other
Musings

A Beginning

The first step is always the hardest.
It really doesn't matter how far it is.
The only thing that is certain about it,
Not taken at all feels very like the end.

Poetry and Verse

A poet is someone who writes poetry.
I don't know what to call someone who writes verse
Which is not up to poetic grade –
Maybe versifier.

It's easy to understand that all verse
Certainly is not poetry – probably most.
That's using the simple understanding of poetry
As verse that other people can enjoy.

The most important reason to versify
Probably has nothing to do with attempting poetry.
For some of us, it is simply the best way to
Express thoughts to ourselves that need expressing.

I would guess there may be as much poetry
Buried in heaps of private verse in attics
As there is verse in anthologies of published poets –
Maybe a good deal more – but it's no loss.

The poet, like any artist needs students in
Order to be judged and have his message understood.
Verse serves its purpose when it is reduced to paper,
And most of it should not see the light of day.

The Light

The Light is there, I know.

Other folks see and talk about it.

Much in word and song is written.

I guess everybody has to find their own switch.

Musing on Time

When I was young – long ago –
I did not think on things enough.
My Daddy, or someone, taught me
That you learn by thinking on things.
I believed, but didn't do enough.

During my middle years I was
Too busy to think on things enough.
Middle years are great for learning too,
But habits get in the way of thinking on things,
And stifle growth and real enjoyment.

Now, in my dotage, I am taking time
To think on things. Daddy was right.
Even with poorer eyesight, weaker legs, etc.
Thinking on things opens all kinds of doors
Even if it is just to go out and smell the roses.

High Places

Driving through mountains reminds me,
Of all things, of being on an ocean liner.
You can see so far to things you'll never see.

When you have climbed to the highest reaches,
Of highway, mountain passes, the distant sights
Are no more distinct than, on ocean, far-off beaches.

To leave the road in the mountains, for a neophyte,
Is almost as dangerous as to jump overboard
From a ship at sea in the middle of the night.

There is a tiredness from both kinds of travel
That lets one sleep in deep repose
So that cares and worries truly unravel.

The Fox

Can you see the fox in the bush?
He's looking back at us, looking at him.
Do you suppose he sees me more clearly?
I find him indistinct, unless he moves.

So much I find like looking at fox in bush.
By the time something comes clear in view
The observer is being observed, so that
It is never clear which is mirror or reality.

Spring Flowers

Spring buds are so pretty.

The first are the best!

I guess it's a lot like kisses.

Making Steel

Many people harden themselves
So that they will not feel the world's bumps,
Forgetting that steeling feelings
Modifies pleasure as well as pain.

Minnesota Winter

Minnesota winters are fun and exciting,

If you like cold and snow for a long time.

November is dark brown until Thanksgiving

When everything turns white with snow.

White Christmases are a regular thing

With steady cold starting a couple of weeks before.

January is thirty-one days of cold and snow

But with bright sunshine most of the time.

February is four weeks more of the same.

The heaviest snow falls in March, but the

Sun is warmer and hints of things to come.

April sees the end of white and turns to green.

Minnesota winters are fun and exciting,

If you like cold and snow for a long time!

The White Stuff

I looked at the snow.

All I could see was mess,

Which reminded me of

The people who hear noise

When music is playing,

And find gibberish and

No meaning in poetry, and

See only burrs and insects

In a garden of flowers, and

Feel an interest in art a waste.

So, I decided to look again

At the beautiful winter scene

Of which the snow was a part.

Musing on mirrors

I looked in a mirror. Someone like me looked back.
I could tell by looking, that if I didn't do something,
My hair would stay a mess. No one had to say a word.
Messy hair isn't very important, yet I would not go out
without checking.

Wrong attitude is a serious deficiency for each
and everyone.
If only there were something like a mirror that would
show a mess inside the head. Then I could beware
Of bad attitude, just as I do appearance of my hair.

There is no easy way to check one's own head.
Maybe it's like a society before mirrors for hair.
I still must try to appear as well as I possibly can,
Even if it is not easy to check the attitude daily, I must.

Oceans Are Long and Flat

The ocean surely does look long and flat.
It looks even longer and flatter than Dakota wheat fields.

It changes one's whole perspective on long and flat,
Especially when you come from the landlocked,
Mostly flat American Midwest.

Not that long and flat are so important everywhere.
They certainly are on the ocean and prairie.

Impression

I remember once I saw something
That had great significance for me.
The next time I happened on to it
I couldn't remember what it was.

Today was a dear

Today was a dear

Not animal

More like a friend

Wish you were here.

The Big Lake

Lake Superior is a great big lake.
It looks a lot like an ocean.
From the shore you can't see the other side.
Weather along the shore is guided by lake.

Hard to believe just a couple miles inland
The temperature is 10 to 20 degrees different
Any time of the year. Today it was $55°$
At the cabin door and $75°$ on top of the hill.

Memorial Day weekend is not the best
Time to judge the refrigerator effect, but
In the cold months – hah – it is
Warmer on the shore than on the hill.

The fulltime residents say you can tell where
A person lives by the length of their sleeves.
That's how it is on the shore of a big lake
Where you can't even see to the other side.

Growing Things

Spring in Minnesota is good for growing things.
After long winter of absence or hibernation,
It's good time for animals and vegetation.

Right after the birds come back from the south
The leaves start coming out on the trees,
And the shrubs and flowers begin to bloom.

The spring sun is particularly good for kids.
They grow well at that time of year,
Just like most other living things around.

As the days get longer and the weather warmer,
Everyone and everything want to be in the sun.
Spring in Minnesota is good for growing things.

The Noise of Color

Most of the time I can wear the clothes
I put on in the morning all day long.

But sometimes, before I get out the door,
my wife hears what I'm wearing,
Even prior to seeing me,
And points out the mismatch of my garb.

There is never a doubt on this issue.
My eye is notorious for its
Inability to see what colors should
Properly be worn in combination.

Though my eye has not improved, my ear
Has learned, sometimes, to hear the clash.
Then, before she calls out to me, I
Have changed, before she even sees me!

Grass

Green is like the grass in May.

It looks so nice,

when properly cut and manicured.

In May the green grass grows fast,

     which requires cutting.

Brown is like the grass in August.

It looks awful,

but doesn't need much cutting or care.

Beauty being in the eye of the beholder,

     August grass is nicer.

March Snowstorm

There is a special thing about
A March snowstorm in Minnesota.

I suppose it's much the same
In other snowy places like
Canada, Michigan, Maine,
Russian Siberia and so forth.

Such a snow fall may be like the
One in November, where the white
Covers the brown landscape of fall,
Because previous snow had melted.

Or it just may add a fresh white
Coat on top of the greying mass
Which had gathered over the whole
of the long suffering winter.

The very special thing about
A March snowstorm in Minnesota,
And those other snowy places, is
That it won't be around for long!

Patience

A long time ago, when I was younger,
An old man, probably younger than I am now,
Told me that the most worthwhile virtue
For leadership in business, in his judgement,
was patience.

At the time, he stated that I might not
understand, and I didn't.

Sometime, along the way, I realized it's truth.
The longer I live the more valuable the lesson.
Now, however, I believe it has application for
Success in life in all aspects, as well as a good trait
for business.

Now I tell young people that truth and hope they
understand what I didn't.

Dead Ends

A great philosopher once said,
"Don't look up a dead horse's ass unless
You want to go into veterinary medicine."
That isn't said very nicely or sweetly,
But the point could not be made more clearly.

People, all of us folks, spend too much
Time on dead ends that should have been buried.
The only legitimate excuse for occupying
Oneself with a past opportunity, is the
Erroneous belief that there still might be life.

I think smart people don't find better
Opportunities than the rest of us.
They just have a quicker read on failure.
The quicker diagnosis gives them the
Chance to move on to living possibilities.

The more I think about it, the more I
Come to believe that saying something nicely
Isn't nearly as important as being understood.
"Don't look up a dead horse's ass unless
You want to go into veterinary medicine."

Promises

A couple months ago I said
I would collect for the Heart Fund.
It's a very useful charity which
Does lots of things that need doing.

Now, a couple of months have passed.
It's time to solicit the neighborhood.
Remind me please – what is the heart fund
Goodness that requires my leisure today?

Windy Days

Windy days are pleasant
In spring or summer.
In spring they dry the rain.
In summer they relieve the heat.

In winter time wind is a threat.
It makes cold days uncomfortable.
With snow or sleet wind creates
An element of danger called blizzard.

Fall windy days don't matter.
The good of spring and summer
Aren't necessary in autumn, and
Dangers of winter don't exist.

The good and bad of windy days
Balance out over twelve months,
But they are absolutely necessary
for young folks flying kites.

My old Daddy taught me

My old Daddy taught me that a fellow who knows his abilities can go a long way, but that a fellow who knows his limitations may be even better prepared.

Dead Leaves

In the fall, colored leaves are pretty
Before and after they drop from trees.

After snow-melt in the spring, dead leaves
Are a mess that must be raked and hauled.

There is a message in the saga
Of tree leaves from fall to haul.

Life

Homo sapiens need food, water and air to exist.

Homo sapiens need love and beauty to live.

A beacon

A beacon in the night to give direction and hope

A signal of day's end without accomplishment

A starting place for study of the universe

A single light not distinguishable to most who look

A whatever for, whomever for, whenever

They walked down the street together

They walked down the street together.

At a corner, each went a different way.

Always the question –

Will they meet again?

Printed in the USA
CPSIA information can be obtained
at www.ICGtesting.com
JSHW080001150824
68134JS00021B/2216

9 781961 884151